Cover design by the a

Cover photography by
https://www.instagr
kylemurrayphotogra]
https://www.kylemurrayphotography.com

# WHAT IS ADVENTURE TO YOU?

*It's your choice.*

How adventure is defined is completely unique to each individual. For some, it could be going for an easy hike near their home, walking around taking pictures of cool trees or taking a new route to work, while for others it may be scaling a mountain in the snow or going on multi-day wildcamping treks.

Adventure doesn't have to involve risk, fear, money, travel, lots of gear, a huge physical exertion or learning a bunch of new things. Forget what your idea of an adventurer may be and don't judge your own outdoors ambitions against folk you see online or know personally as that is *their* journey, not yours.

You are about to become an incredible, as capable as you want to be adventurer, as you define the pillars and an action plan for *your* new outdoors life.

Found Outside is an Adventure Audit programme in which you will create a completely custom-to-you adventure life which involves only the outdoor activities you feel comfortable with, are capable of and that fits into your life.

Note: this book will focus mainly, though not exclusively on the adventures of hiking, camping, walking and mountaineering.

# ABOUT THE AUTHOR.

*@TheTartanHiker (Instagram, YouTube, TikTok, Facebook, Twitch, Patreon.*

The following may seem like 'too much information', but I feel it's important for you to get to know who I am and my journey to this point so you can understand that I have experience behind every piece of advice I give.

I'm Paul MacIntyre, an adventure coach and outdoors content creator known as 'The Tartan Hiker', from Glasgow in Scotland. My personal adventure journey started in difficult circumstances. As a child growing up in poverty-ridden council estates in North Glasgow, I was forced to find adventure outside to not only escape a challenging home-life, but to create free entertainment. In my young years, I experienced and saw things no child should ever have to.

While the young people around me put on tough exteriors and became rough, fighting 'scheme boys' – I chose to create elaborate adventures for myself in the outdoors as a way of escapism. Even though I was the biggest kid in school and had a father who insisted I become a 'gangster' like him, I was what he would constantly call a 'wee shitebag'. I was a sensitive kid who was pretty much scared of everything and to be honest still am. Whenever I share stories, photos, or content from my adventures, people often comment on how brave and confident I must be, when the truth is I'm absolutely terrified a lot of the time. There is not a more apt saying than 'if I can do it, anyone can'.

In those early days I would walk for miles around Glasgow, pushing the boundaries of my wee legs and mind. It sounds unthinkable nowadays, but back then, parents would literally tell their kids to get out of the house after breakfast and not come back until it got dark, with no clue as to where they were or what they were up to. I would walk for hours on end, climb huge spiked fences and walls, break into buildings to look around, hike over vast fields and hills, set fires, dig up coal (the area I lived until seven was called 'Milton' and was built on an abandoned coal mine), cross rivers, steal food from shops to fuel the hike home, climb castle ruins, get chased by farm German Shepards and (usually) make it home just in time for the street lights coming on. When home and trying to deal with the fear and constant anxiety caused by my surroundings, I would create a vivid fantasy world where I was an Indiana Jones-type explorer finding treasure and adventure in faraway lands.

My mother was living her life in a fantasy world similar to myself. My controlling father wouldn't let her work, have friends or leave the house for anything other than shopping or visiting my grandmother, so she lived her adventure life by reading books exclusively about adventurers and travellers going on epic, trailblazing odysseys, then would fascinate me with their stories. She (and therefore I) would watch TV shows such as Michael Palin's 'Around the World in 80 Days' and documentaries about weird and wonderful foreign lands. When going to the few permitted places we were allowed by my father to visit, she would take me on indulgent, elaborate routes through areas we'd never been in, taking in the sights and sounds of new places. My dad would be told we were getting the bus, but she would instead walk myself and my little brother for many miles to our destination and buy us sweets and comics with the money. I truly owe my entire adventure life to my mum. It was then that the seeds were planted for a life of exploration.

My childhood adventures extended into my teen years and twenties as I enjoyed expanding my knowledge and efforts in the outdoors, but eventually working life, coupled with analysis paralysis and too much partying stopped me in my tracks. I was desperate to restart my adventure journey but had no-idea where or how to start. I spent a few years depressed and desperate, simply walking the streets of Glasgow for sometimes forty or fifty miles at a time.

My mum died in 2013 at only 51 years old when her alcoholism consumed her. I didn't want a stranger hosting the ceremony, so I took the role. No matter the challenge of any adventure I've ever done, nothing will compare to the mental effort it took to hold it together and not cry for the duration of the service and day, determined as I was to not break for my younger brother's sake. Not only did I manage to not cry that day, I didn't cry again until almost a decade later when the gravity of her death finally hit home.

Following my mum's death, I took my adventure life to an extreme level. I spent the next ten years from 2013 to 2023 on a mission to silence my pain with punishing adventure. I walked across entire countries, spent wild nights in dangerous situations, sought out near death outdoor experiences, climbed over a thousand mountains, ran ultramarathons, marathons and went on treks until the soles of my feet literally rubbed off. Anything easy was unacceptable. The day after I fell onto a sharp spike from a fencepost which went right through my knee, I ran for 36 miles over 25,000 feet of mountains in minus 10-degree weather. I spent the entire day in tears from the pain, only to fall and tear open my other knee before pissing myself. Covered in blood, urine and tears, I planned my next week of adventure in the car park and returned the next week for more torture.

I needed to feel pain, or it simply wasn't worth it. A 4:41 minute mile, not good enough – faster! A 3:13 marathon – faster! I kept looking for new ways to punish myself in the way of 'growth'. I would run marathons in summer with no water or sugar gels, go on fifty-mile hikes across vast areas with no navigation aids, water or food. I eliminated everything I thought was harmful and/or unproductive. I became vegan, teetotal, stopped watching tv, playing videos games and eliminated anything which brought me joy as I craved the kind of pain which I could only get from extreme adventures and physical punishment. My unnecessary elite-athlete fitness levels and emaciated six-foot one, 146-pound body were never enough. It seems so obvious now I was covering up the fact I was a devastated wee boy who couldn't handle that his mum was dead, so chose to block it out with pain.

It was during this period I became a full-time adventure coach. As an adventure coach, I help plan adventures into my clients' lives, keep them on track, advise them how, check in on them, plan Scottish holidays, consult on gear and more –

like a personal trainer but for adventure. This was something I had been dreaming up and juggling around in my head since 2011, which I thought was just a silly dream. It became one of those dreams which would not go away and tapped on my shoulder endlessly. I can recall the *exact* moment I finally figured out how I would at least try to make it possible. I was descending a mountain in Luss called, 'Beinn Dubh' for the third time that month when it felt like I was given the thumbs-up by my own soul.

My job at the time and since 2006 was as a musician. I was a guitarist playing on studio recordings, live stand-in, wedding bands, teaching and would sell guitars and courses online. As cool as it may sound, it was only fun for the first two years until it became just another job I resented. All I wanted was to be hiking, running and enjoying the outdoors. My time as a guitarist led me to know a lot of people with all-consuming, high-income jobs who were stressed out and feeling trapped, desperate for adventure. A certain number of these clients would be keen for the session to end so they could ask about my adventures. It was this which lay the seed of becoming a coach to these very people. I had been in their shoes, I knew what it was like to crave adventure but not know where to start and be overwhelmed by the options and requirements. On May 27$^{th}$, 2016, I emailed eleven of these clients with a proposal to be their adventure coach and get them back outdoors and into a life of adventure and excitement, parallel to their busy home lives. Of the eleven people I emailed, all eleven immediately agreed. One email had changed the trajectory of my life and almost doubled my monthly income overnight. In October of that year, once my guitar commitments were honoured, I was now a fully-fledged, full-time adventure coach.

When Covid arrived, I was forced to adventure closer to home in the lowlands of Scotland, just as

I had before I tried to numb the pain with intense excursions far from home. I was initially crushed but soon fell back in love with making the best of what was close and not seeing it as 'less-than'. I was home more; my coaching business was thriving, and I was finally learning that I don't need to annihilate myself to enjoy the outdoors. Just as I was achieving my dream in these areas, it seemed to allow time and space for me to finally realise something – my mum was dead. I don't know if it's common for mourning someone's death to take eight years, but well, my mum had never died before. I had a complete mental breakdown as if my mum had just passed away the day before. I was no-longer covering up the truth by making my pain so loud I couldn't hear it.

In the process of trying to recover, I attended private medical specialists to try and diagnose a long-term health issue, which one month later had me staring at a scan of the inside of my head as a neurosurgeon informed me I had a brain tumour on my pituitary gland. I started seeing a psychiatrist and was diagnosed as suffering from severe childhood trauma (CPTSD), ADHD and autism. My psychiatrist suggested the childhood trauma test results where the worst he'd ever seen and seemed genuinely shocked. Although I was already in the throes of a mental breakdown, the news of the tumour and mental health diagnoses came at the best time as everything became somewhat of a blur, and on reflection dealing with everything at once was better than having to try and deal with each individual disaster over a longer period. I began to slowly understand and heal my mental health issues and be thankful that the growth in my brain remains stable.

On July 2$^{nd}$, 2024, exactly a year before I released this book you are reading now, I started making content on the subject of teaching what I know to beginner and aspiring hikers. I knew all-to-well how hard it is to crave adventure but struggle to get started, and how important it is to seek solace in the outdoors to help mitigate the pain of mental health troubles. I decided I was going to give absolutely everything to making sure people like me, who I was and who I am had someone to turn to for help.

Nothing has brought me more joy than the literal thousands of people who have got in touch to say I have helped them get started, improved their adventure journey and who enjoy watching me show off Scotland's beauty. I feel truly honoured to be in a position where people look to me for guidance and entertainment.

I am truly honoured to be your adventure coach.

Now let's create your perfect adventure life!

# INTRODUCTION.

*You can and will have adventure in your life, no matter your circumstances.*

As an adventure coach, I've encountered hundreds of people who crave adventure yet let their self-inflicted or perceived limitations keep them dreaming from their couch as they sigh at some influencer's post (maybe even one of mine), thinking of what could be, but having no idea where to start.

The Found Outside Adventure Audit is a programme I developed over the past nine years to guide my coaching clients to where they need to be. It has been put into action countless times by many struggling outdoors dreamers.

I want to make clear from the very beginning of this book that you are about to embark on *your* adventure journey, no-one else's. The process of the

Adventure Audit will filter down to exactly what is genuinely possible in order to arrive at an honest, real starting point for your journey. You are about to embark on an adventure reality check to set you on a path which is genuinely achievable for the ability and resources you have available.

*A dream will forever stay a dream if it is impossible.*

You will have to let go of, modify and reassess some or maybe even all of your adventure dreams and aspirations if your lifestyle and circumstances won't allow it. A dream will forever stay a dream if it is impossible. You will now design your adventure life based on what can truly be achieved with as much or as little effort as you wish or can commit. It may seem a tad depressing at first when you realise you can't in fact do everything you've fantasised about doing, but rest-assured once the smoke has cleared from the initial reality-check stage, you will then have a clear path to making an achievable life of adventure a reality.

First, we will raise to the ground, then we will build.

It's time to get found outside.

# HOW TO USE THIS BOOK.

*Cut, keep or change.*

Found Outside is a workbook which requires you to take notes throughout as we embark on a journey together to design your perfect adventure life. You'll need a notebook or journal to write down your answers and goals. You can complete the Adventure Audit in whichever way you find works best for you - in as little as few hours from start to finish or by tackling a chapter/exercise one at a time. The book is designed to be concise and to-the-point. Less time reading, more time adventuring!

At the end of each section, you will find a list of questions you should answer and take notes on, with example answers given for each. These answers will be essential to setting your goals and creating actionable plans.

The most important part of your Adventure Audit is deciding if you should CUT, KEEP or CHANGE any goals based on the answers and realities you uncover, as explained further below:

CUT:

You must pick apart whatever goals you set and look for reasons not why you think you *could* achieve them, but reasons why you think or know you *couldn't*. You must filter out dreams from goals. If the noes are the clear majority over yeses – it's time to cut the goals from your plans **for now.**

KEEP:

If you find overwhelming reasons why you *could* achieve a goal, but not many or even any reasons why you possibly *couldn't* – you will have an achievable goal you can get to work on actioning. You have a solid goal to work toward.

CHANGE:

When there's a close balance between noes and yeses, you've discovered a goal which won't work in its current form and should therefore be modified to fit into the parameters uncovered as you complete your Adventure Audit. Change to make it fit, but if you still can't, it's time to cut.

# ACTION.

1. Get yourself a notebook and pen.

# WHERE ARE YOU NOW?

*There are no levels, only your level.*

This first part of your Adventure Audit is to define and uncover the realities of your current situation. Once you know what you have to improve, what you have available and what you can give to your new plans, only then can you make a true blueprint to work from. Think of the initial chapter as demolishing an old house, removing all the debris and preparing the land to make a solid foundation for the new build to come, built to your exact standards.

This is the beginning of your filtering down to the essence of what is realistically possible for your adventure life, as opposed to what you *think* is possible, while uncovering any roadblocks both real and perceived. The key to not only an amazing life of adventure, but an amazing life in general isn't about what you can add, it's about what you can take away to be left with the very essence of what makes you happy and fulfilled. Although when you complete the Adventure Audit process you may realise what is possible is less than you hoped for; you will be left in a better place to get the best out of what you can do, with a clear focus on your new life.

*Realistic. Attainable. Actionable.*

Every person can live a life of adventure, but every person also has their level. The hardest part for many can be finding that level. Some set too high aspirations, others too little. For example, many clients I work with often cite the same goal – they want to climb every Munro in Scotland (282 mountains over 3000 feet), but when we complete the Adventure Audit we immediately see that it is quite literally impossible given their current and future lifestyle and situations (see the next chapter, 'DO you really want it?'). The beauty of the Adventure Audit is that it sets out what you can realistically achieve from a new amazing life of adventure and steers you from a life of frustration at not being able to achieve something no amount of dreaming can make it a reality.

Regardless of the realities the audit uncovers for you, you can and will have more adventure in your life which works for you. There are no 'levels' or 'better-thans', only *your* level.

We will audit the most important factors in establishing your new baseline:

- Your initial goals
- What you don't you want and why
- The consequences of failure
- Experience
- Health
- Fitness
- Effort and confidence

- Budget
- Time availability
- Location
- Social desires
- If you really want it
- Why you want it

As you progress through the Adventure Audit, you will cut, keep or change your plans as you answer the questions.

# DO YOU REALLY WANT IT?

*Dreams are holding you back.*

*Forget dreams, it's time to filter down to the absolute reality of what is truly possible.*

If you're not sure the rules of the game, you're going to have a tough time playing it. The same goes for your adventure goals. It's too easy to make grand goals and hold onto them like intangible 'I owe you' notes to our future selves. Setting a goal you're hazy on or don't make actionable plans for achieving can lead to your taking your foot off the gas. Just writing it down, thinking about it or worse – telling others, can give you a false sense of having done something toward its achievement. You haven't. A dream you don't take action toward achieving will forever remain a dream. Dreams are worthless as they involve zero effort yet give you a false sense of achievement.

Let's look again at one of the most popular adventure dreams/goals set by countless folk in Scotland. The dream of climbing every Munro:

As mentioned, there are 282 mountains in Scotland over 3,000 feet tall with a drop at each side of at least 500 feet which qualifies them to be deemed 'Munros', therefore making the exclusive list published in 1891, which has since been expanded upon and updated.

As an adventure coach and outdoorsman over three decades, I have come across literally hundreds of folk who express their dream to climb every Munro, yet have only met three who have managed it. In the almost 150 years since the list was published, only around 7,700 people have actually done it according to the 'Munro Society', where 'compleaters' (the term given to those who do so) register their achievement to receive a certificate.

It is of course a noble and thrilling goal to set but is one most people will never be able to achieve due to the factual realities of their life situation and what father time puts in their way. Someone with the dream of climbing every Munro would have to look at the realities ahead to determine if it's possible, which is what you will be doing with every goal you set in your Adventure Audit.

Use the following example as a guide on how you should approach your adventure goal setting. You must be a realist, pessimist and a true conservative. You can without question achieve great things, but we are here to make sure you only set the goals which are genuinely possible to your unique situations. Some goals can and should seem a little out of reach, make you nervous and question if you can really achieve them, but you should know in your heart that with proper resolve and growth – you can get there. Setting silly goals you know deep-down or even on the surface you can never truly achieve or will be very unlikely, will only serve to frustrate and depress you. As your adventure goals and life continue to grow, you can redo this audit down the line and make grander goals with your newfound experiences and confidence.

The following is an example of how you should approach determining if the facts and requirements required for pursuing your goals are realistically achievable. These harsh realities push you to uncover not only if the steps and sacrifices you will need to make are achievable, but if you really are willing to give what is needed, based on your desired commitment level.

First, look at the facts and realities for what will be required in the pursuit and execution of your goal, then ask yourself if you are truly willing and able to do what would be required.

**An example of how to question and test your goals:**

## Climbing every Munro

Facts:

As a conservative estimate it will take around 150 to 170 days of mountaineering, summiting multiple Munros on the same day for many of those days. You would have to add on days for overnight stays and sometimes intricate, sometimes rough travel plans, adding around 100 days for travel and overnight stays to areas with difficult access and zero public transport links for many/most. Overnight stays would be required for many in the form of camping or by accommodation which can be hard to find or get availability, especially in non-winter months.

Questions:

- Days required are around 250. Can you give this number of days to the goal?
- Can you get the time off from work?
- Can you get childcare if needed?
- Can you afford the travel and accommodation?

- If you can only give one weekend a month to mountaineering, are you okay with the goal possibly taking twenty years? (which is fine!)
- Do you drive? If not, how will you get to some of the most remote parts of Scotland and if you do are you comfortable driving on rough, single-track, unmaintained roads?

Facts:

If you want to mitigate the much higher risks of winter mountaineering by climbing in the spring and summer months to take advantage of the better weather, chances of good views and longer days, you are also accepting a daily battle with our dreaded wee beasties! Insects can make travel in Scotland an incredibly uncomfortable experience from April to Late September in many areas.

Questions:

- Can you handle being literally attacked

by swarming black clouds of midges every morning and evening?

- Are you willing to deal with the high chance of being regularly bitten by cleggs which cause incredibly painful, swollen rashes which make you scratch uncontrollably as well as the high chance of having to deal with removing ticks which could cause lyme disease? (I know two people who can no-longer climb hills or enjoy life as they used to due to tick-induced lyme disease which caused ever-lasting side-effects.)
- Are you okay with spraying toxic chemicals on your skin to help mitigate insect bites as well as wear a face net?

Facts:

The weather will ruin your plans more than you could imagine, which alongside making your journeys far more dangerous, will result in not being able to enjoy the amazing views usually on offer. It is not a question of *if* the weather changes your plans or makes your days less desirable and more dangerous, it's a matter of *when.* It's guaranteed.

Questions:

- Are you happy to complete a large number of Munros without seeing any views?
- Do you mind hiking in horizontal rain, battering winds and being covered by cloud for hours and days on end?
- Are you competent enough as a navigator to get yourself to safety should your electronics die? (you should of course never rely solely on tech).

Facts:

The odds of completing this epic journey without getting hurt at least once are relatively slim. You must be a competent mountaineer and be able to deal with the many extremely dangerous situations wild Scotland presents you with.

Questions:

- There is a chance you could get seriously injured, are you willing to take that risk?
- You might die trying, just as many unfortunate souls have. Are you okay with this risk?
- Are you happy to risk your life which could leave your family at home without you?
- Do you have the appropriate gear and safety knowledge?
- Can your family afford to maintain their lifestyle should you get seriously injured or die?
- Can you afford the increased insurance costs a mountaineer will incur?
- Do you know how to deal with an injury suffered in the mountains?
- Can you find your way to safety if you get lost?
- Specialist gear (and knowledge) is required for certain Munros, as well as hired guides for mountains such as the Cuillins on The Isle of Skye. Can you afford these essentials?

This example could go on with more questions in regard to budget, fitness (and all subjects covered in the Adventure Audit), but I'm sure you understand by now that it is simply a process of getting more 'yeses' than 'noes' in deciding if your goal is realistically possible.

Remember to not focus on finding reasons why you *could* achieve your goals – try to find every possible reason why you *couldn't*. If you cannot find enough reasons why you can't do it, congratulations, you have a winner!

# SET YOUR INITIAL GOALS.

*Let's get started.*

The Adventure Audit will guide you to create a realistic set of incredible goals with actionable steps, but for now, it's time to get down on paper everything you think you would like to achieve, regardless of how far-fetched or seemingly out of reach it may seem.

*Beware long-term goals.*

People often get carried away by setting 'someday' goals which it seems okay to just put out there and never take action toward as they are so far in the future. Therefore, try to focus on mostly goals which you can achieve within near-term (such as a year) to at most three years. You should set goals which can be acted upon in even the smallest way NOW. Your Adventure Audit will get you adventuring **immediately**.

Once you get into living a more adventurous life, you may find your desires shift and end up craving something different than the long-term goals you set in the past. Long-term goals can also be counterproductive as they can often blur goals in the shorter term as you feel everything must serve these future, immovable pillars. Concentrating on what you want from the upcoming year or so keeps your feet on the ground and will give you the satisfaction of achievement in the nearer term.

As you set your adventure goals below, be sure to also include fitness, health and body goals (such as weight loss, strength gain, muscle gain and such), as they and adventure outdoors are forever linked. Also include 'thing goals' such as gear.

Be sure to completely empty your mind of every last thing you can think you would like to do, achieve or get into until you simply can't think of anything else. Have a complete brain dump – there are no wrong answers at this point!

# EXERCISE 1.

## Brain Dump Every Single Possible Goal You Can Think Of.

a. Take as much time as you need to list every single adventure goal you can think you may like to do. From something you may have been dreaming of for a long time, to a tiny idea you think may be cool.

See the below example for ideas of the kind of goals you should set:

- Go on a solo hike

- Three-day wildcamp in the mountains of Glencoe

- Lose ten pounds of fat to make hiking easier

- Buy a bicycle and pannier

- Climb ten mountains over 2000 feet

# WHY DO YOU WANT IT?

*The key to success is asking why over and over again.*

Whenever you have a goal you want to achieve, an important first step is to understand *why* you want to achieve it. 'That's easy' you may think. 'I want to win the lottery so I can have loads of money'... WHY do you want loads of cash? To buy stuff? Why do you want that stuff? ... After you ask why until you can't anymore, you will get to the root reason you want the goal, which in the case of winning the lottery could eventually be 'because I want to feel safe and take care of my family'. From here you can see what you really want and make a proper plan to achieve it, rather than an outlandish, never-gonna-happen dream like winning the lottery.

When you keep asking why until you can't anymore, you peel back the layers to get to the real answer, digging deep even beyond the bullshit you tell yourself inside your head. You dig to the core. You get to the very essence of why you want to achieve an adventure goal and the process of eliminating vague or confused motivations helps decide if you actually want to go through with it or if it's just masking a desire for something else. We are very quick to set huge goals, when they in fact may harbour a small seed of what you really want buried deep inside. (Do you want to climb every Munro, or do you just want to see some sights around Scotland…?) A lot of people have the desire to endlessly travel the world, as did I. I would set ridiculous goals such as hiking around the planet, cycling from coast to coast on every continent, working my way around the world on cargo ships, etc – when I knew I didn't actually want to leave Scotland! The truth at the front line of my desires to 'run away from it all' was depression at my current life, caused by a lifetime of not dealing with childhood trauma and at the time undiagnosed ADHD and autism. What I really wanted was adventure, a change of scene, a little danger, to be fulfilled, set on a purposeful path, meet a girl to spend my life with and get outside my comfort zone now and then. I'm sure you know people who say they just 'wanna get away from this shithole', when what they really want is a happier life of purpose. The problem with dreaming of 'getting away' is summed up perfectly by my psychiatrist who says, 'Wherever you go, there you are.'

The following example will pick apart a long-held goal by asking why over and again to get to the route of what the person truly wants and why:

**Goal: I want to walk from Land's End to John O'Groat's**

Why do I want to walk from Land's End to John O'Groats?

*Because I want a grand adventure.*

Why do I want a grand adventure?

*It would just be cool.*

Why would it be cool?

*I would get to see Britain.*

Why, what do you want to see?

*Just... All of it!*

Why can't you name anything you want to see in particular?

*It's not really about what I'll see it's more for the challenge.*

Why do you want a challenge?

*I'm bored and want to do something big.*

Why are you bored?

*All I do is work.*

Why don't you like your work?

*It gives me no time for me.*

Why do you want more time for you?

*Because I miss going adventures like I used to when I was at university.*

Why don't you go on adventures like you used to?

*Because I'm always working!*

Why, do you work on weekends?

*No, but I'm so tired all I have time to do is catch up on life admin.*

You eventually narrow down to the ultimate answer and possible action steps which could be taken to cut, keep or change the goal. Be sure to ask why at least **five** times en route to finding your core answer (For further reading, research 'The five whys model' online).

**True answer and plan:** I'm tired, miss not going on adventures like I used to and am overworked. I dreamed of a massive adventure when in fact I now realise I barely go on any small ones, never mind a huge one like this. I just want to feel adventurous again. I need to make a plan to work on getting my career and adventure life in balance more, so will start looking at ways to make that happen without a drastic, temporary fix.

Dig deep to uncover if your epic goals are in fact your way of communicating a lack in other unrelated areas of your life which need addressed.

Note: Even if you get to the root answer which proves you really do want the goal, it may still not be possible due to other factors, (such as time availability, budget etc...), but you will at least uncover if it's something you really want to achieve.

# EXERCISE 2.

## Getting To The Root Reason For Why You Set These Goals.

Based on the answers you give, decide if you should cut, keep or change any goals.

    a.  Go through each goal from your list and ask yourself WHY you want to achieve it or like the sound of it. Keep asking why until you can't anymore – it will lead you to the source of your desire for said goal. You may write your reasons down or simply ponder your why answers.

# EXPERIENCE.

*Finding your baseline.*

To figure out where your starting point may be for your new goals, we will first unpack what experiences you've have had which could lend to the areas you want to get into.

## **No Experience.**

No experience is necessary to start whatever type of adventures you desire at a certain level. If, for example, you wanted to get into mountaineering, you probably shouldn't just head up a mountain, but there are ways you can get started at a lower level (literally). No-one starts with experience, so don't worry if your new goals involve doing or learning things you've never done.

# EXERCISE 3.1.

## Goals You'll Be Starting From Scratch With Zero Experience.

Skip this exercise if you have experience in any of your goals.

a. Review your goals list for the things you want to do but have no experience in and write them down on a new list.

Examples answers:

- Paddleboarding

- Cycle touring

- Weightlifting

- Foreign adventure

## **A Little Experience.**

Having a little experience can also be a hindrance. Clients I've had who have experience can often find it difficult to change their ways and accept they must modify how they do things. If you have recent experience and the aim of your taking this Adventure Audit is to streamline your journey and get on-path, you can absolutely start on a higher level than a total beginner, but if your experience was quite long ago, you may benefit from approaching the endeavour as if a beginner. Being humble and accepting of restarting your journey will give you a clearer path to your adventure promised land.

# EXERCISE 3.2.

## Goal Ideas You Have At Least A Little Experience In.

Skip this exercise if you don't have a little experience in any of the goals you've set, (but I bet you'll uncover something!)

a. Review your goals list for the things you want to do which you have a little experience in and write them down on a new list.

Example:

A little experience: Hiking

b. From the new list, write down every useful skill you have from that little experience which could be used in toward your new goals.

Example:

Skills which can help other goals:

- Following a route, packing the correct gear, driving country roads, using GPS…

## **Lots Of Experience.**

Sometimes experience can bring analysis paralysis and/or an inability to accept less than you are capable of or used to doing. Quite often I deal with clients who have a huge amount of experience in disciplines such as mountaineering, hiking, ultra running, and cycling, but their lives have become so busy they can no-longer factor their outdoors hobby into their life or have become bored with the same old routine. They then come to me for a re-evaluation and guidance on what to do next. It's not just those who are beginning their journey who need a brutal reality check to audit what's possible, it's also the most experienced.

# EXERCISE 3.3.

## Goal Ideas You Have A Lot Of Experience In.

Skip this exercise if you don't have a lot of experience in any of your desired goals.

a. Review your goals list for pursuits you have a lot of experience in and transfer them to a new list.

Example:

A lot of experience: Running

b. From the new list, write down every useful skill you have from your wealth of experience which could be used in toward your new goals.

Example:

Skills which can help other goals: (Running)

Developed good ankle strength, pacing, training to a schedule, endurance, nutrition…

# WHAT YOU DON'T WANT AND WHY.

*Set yourself up to win.*

Perhaps the single most important thing in your adventure planning will be eliminating what you don't want to do. This includes things you feel you should or could do, but don't really want to. Everyone has to do certain things they don't want to as there's sometimes no choice, so what you must learn to do is say no to the things you *can* say no to which don't appeal to you.

*The key to consistent adventure outdoors is making sure you go all-in on the things you know you'll enjoy while minimising or ideally eliminating that which you don't.*

Also bear in mind you may think you don't want to do something as you haven't tried it or had a bad experience in the past, so you should be willing to test the waters to see if your opinion still holds true. To use myself as an example, I convinced myself I hated camping after I done Land's End to John O'Groats (the entire length of Great Britain), wild camping the entire 1,200 mile-ish journey. For three years I had the horrible memories of so many brutal camps in my mind and so avoided camping completely. A few years later, I had a vision of a long-distance hike which had no accommodation or chance of completion in a day. I had no choice, but to camp. What followed was the most amazing, reinvigorating trek which rekindled my love for wildcamping.

This may sound obvious, but if there's things you know you don't like and can avoid doing them – consider them cut! If you don't like hiking in the rain, don't hike when it's raining or is scheduled to. If you don't like anything longer than an hour, don't do anything longer than an hour. If you don't want to drive for more than thirty minutes, that's your boundary. It's all about not setting yourself up to fail... Set yourself up to win!

This is your journey which is completely unique to you. It matters not what other people are willing to put up with or the lengths they'll go to – this is the YOU show!

# EXERCISE 4.

## Decide What You Don't Want.

Based on the answers you give, decide if you should cut, keep, or change any goals.

a. Make a list of everything you want to avoid from your adventure journey. Write two columns; What you would like to avoid if possible, and non-negotiables you insist on avoiding.

Example:

Avoid if possible: Rain, midges, hills that start with an immediate incline.

Avoid non-negotiable: Long drives, heights, activities longer than four hours.

b. Now list ways you could possibly get around or avoid these things.

How avoid them: (rain) Only go when weather forecast is clear. (heights) Stick to low level trail or hills with no sharp drops…

# THE CONSEQUENCES OF FAILURE.

*Hell is meeting the person you could've become.*

The pain of not achieving something can linger for the rest of your life, becoming a thorn in your side and a constant reminder that you never lived up to your potential. The pain however, is easier to take if you at least tried.

The goal of this chapter is to create a glance into the future at how you will feel if you don't take action on the plans you are creating in your Adventure Audit and therefore don't achieve them. You've obviously been drawn to this book as you were unsatisfied with your adventure life and wanted help and guidance to get on the right path, so ask yourself how you would feel if years pass and you still haven't attempted to make your goals a reality.

Everything you do now should be for your future self, for that 'auld yin' ('old person' in Scottish). Imagine being eighty years old and being full of regrets at having never achieved your outdoor goals. Now imagine the satisfaction and memories you will have at that age as you look back at a life fully lived and experienced.

You don't need to look so far in the future. When Christmas comes and goes this year or next, imagine how you will feel when you watch yet another year pass without living a life you know you want.

Procrastination eventually turns into loss.

# EXERCISE 5.

## The Long-Term Cost Of Not Taking Action.

Based on the answers you give, decide if you should cut, keep or change any goals.

a. List all the things you don't like about your current situation related to your desired adventures.

Example: Things don't like: 30 pounds overweight, bored, unfit, desperate to go hiking but don't know how, sad when see folk living a life I would love

b. Now add what could happen if you stay on the path you're on now and don't take action in 1, 5, 10, 20 + years year or whichever units of time you wish.

Example:

(30 Pounds overweight) Could be even heavier and suffer from accompanying health conditions.

# HEALTH.

*You can live an adventurous life, no matter your circumstances.*

I was visiting my 77 year-auld granny in a care facility when she told me of her most cherished times as a child. She regaled me with stories of spending her summers in Balmaha in Loch Lomond where she and her family would stay in a converted train cart overlooking the loch.

She beamed as she recalled these memories at if they happened only yesterday. I had never heard the story before, or in fact any story like this from her past as she rarely opened up. She was a notoriously quiet woman who never told stories and was very much a closed book. I asked why she'd never been back to Balmaha to revisit the site of such cherished memories, given that it's only twenty-one miles from where she lived her entire life. She shrugged it off as if it was a ridiculous suggestion. Consumed by arthritis, asthma and a plethora of ails, she was barely able to walk for more than a few minutes. She pointed at her legs as if to say, 'look at me, I'm old, finished and in a care home'.

Nonsense. I told her not only are we going there right now, we're also going to experience Loch Lomond to the fullest and create memories just as cherished as she'd had as a child 70 years ago.

I helped her into my car and we headed to Loch Lomond. I wasn't concerned with what my granny couldn't do, only what she could. Although the converted train was long gone, we had an amazing day in the area. I took her to places where she could appreciate one of the most beautiful places on Earth at her own level and pace. As she couldn't walk much, we drove to the areas with loch-side car parks and stood by the Loch admiring the view. We dined in the famous 'Oak Tree Inn' while looking out at the water, touched trees at the foot of Conic Hill, walked the short boardwalk at Lomond shores, looked through binoculars at the mountains and breathed in the bonnie air which is like a drug to us Scottish. To breathe the air that rises from a loch is to breathe home itself.

She thought she was finished and would never have seen those places again, but this story highlights what I need you to again understand - *you can live an adventurous life, no matter your circumstances.* You can find a level you are capable of. You have to let go of the things you desire which you simply cannot do due to your health, time constraints and other 'road blockers' and instead find and focus on exactly what you can. Whatever you do, as long as you go home happy after having some good times in a situation and surrounding which brings you joy, peace and happiness – you've had a great adventure.

I was hiking in Dunvegan on the Isle of Skye two months later when my granny died. Although we were never that close, we were brought closer that day in Loch Lomond as I saw a seventy-seven year-old-woman who barely said a word to me or showed any signs of affection in all the years I'd known her, absolutely come alive and connect with me through adventure on a visit back in time she thought she would never experience again. I regret not getting to know this side of her when she was still here.

Health issues are the one thing that you may not be able to overcome by working harder or being tough. You must take them very seriously while at the same time knowing it isn't a black mark stopping you from having an adventurous life – you simply have to find a way – and find a way we shall!

If you have no health issues, great – you're good to go in this respect, but if you do it should go without saying that you must consult your doctor to let them know your plans. Just be aware that doctors are notorious for being insanely cautious and perhaps rightly so. As long as you're sensible in respecting your health-induced limitations, you will be capable of way more than you may think.

You will continue to uncover exactly what your adventure parameters are as we progress in the Adventure Audit, with your health realities only being part of, not dominating, a holistic plan for adventure.

The adrenaline at the start of a hike or similar can help you overcome your limitations initially, but when it wears off and your issues get the better of you, you could find yourself in a position where you cannot make it back to safety. If you think this could be you, it should be a crucial factor in determining the type of adventures you can undertake.

The same applies for injuries which you have or are at risk from suffering. Many folk are hindered by injuries from long ago which play-up when trying to do something strenuous. Do not try to push through an injury or put yourself in a position where it could get worse or stop you in your tracks. You must ignore idiots online who preach about running races with broken legs and torn muscles. It's not showing strength and it is not admirable. Everything you do should have a consideration for older you, for you in 10-20 years or more. As someone who has irreversible injuries in his calf and foot from being an ego-laden, screw-the-pain ultramarathon runner and long distance trekker, I wish I could wind the clock back a decade and plead with younger Paul to just stop and rest until he was truly ready.

If you do have health or injury issues, you will need to arrange adventures in which you have options and opportunities to stay safe such as;

- Multiple options to bail, such as bus stops and exits
- Pick-up options
- Rest stops
- Someone to call for help
- Someone to go with
- Popular areas so you can appeal to others for

help if needed
- City/park adventures only
- Car tours...

Also, use trekking poles. Don't argue. It doesn't matter if you're 15 or 75. If you think you don't need them, you're wrong. Just use them. (See chapter: Gear.)

# EXERCISE 6.

## Health Issues Which May Or Will Affect Your Adventure Plans.

Based on the answers you give, decide if you should cut, keep or change any goals.

If you are lucky enough to have no health issues or potential health issues, you can skip this exercise.

    a.    List every health issue which WILL impact your adventure goals:

Example:

Asthma

    b.    List every health issue which MAY impact your adventure goals.

Example:

Knee injury which sometimes

flares up during exercise.

    c.  Now you have the above information, look through you goals list for any which will or may be impacted by health or injury

issues and list ways you can mitigate,
deal with or avoid the risks involved.

Example:

(Asthma)

Stick to easier hikes, visit doctor to
ask for advice and maybe a stronger
'for emergencies' inhaler.

(Knee flare-up)

Always have brace in backpack, work on
strengthening the area, avoid rugged
declines as much as possible.

# FITNESS.

*You're fit enough to get started.*

Do not wait until you are what you deem, 'fit enough' to start adventuring. You *are* fit enough to start going on hikes or whatever you desire to do at your current level of fitness. A lot of what will determine your current level of fitness and what is available to you is very similar to what was put forward in the 'health' subject; such as making sure you can get back, have multiple bail points, easy route, etc (see previous subject 'Health'). The difference is that while you can greatly improve your fitness levels, your health issues may be permanent and unchangeable.

Fitness can be easy to overestimate. I've seen many folk crumble after giving everything they have to reach the summit of a mountain, only to face the devastating reality that they now must now turn around and do the whole thing again in reverse, only now they are devoid of energy, (if you aren't aware, going down a mountain is usually harder than going up).

You must be extra-cautious in determining what you believe your current fitness levels can afford you and give plenty of allowance for being wrong. For example, if you think you can manage a ten-mile hike, make it seven or eight.

It may surprise some, but an important thing to understand is that you do not get hiking fit primarily by hiking. Hiking and adventure fitness should be built off-trail in ways you enjoy, are capable of and which fit into your life, such as walking, running, weightlifting, walking up stairs, gym classes, stretching, etc.

# EXERCISE 7.

## Your Current Fitness Levels And Which Areas Will You Need To Improve On.

Based on the answers you give, decide if you should cut, keep or change any goals.

a. Look through your goals list for those which will require you to improve your fitness and put them into a new two column list, titled; somewhat improve fitness and drastically improve fitness.

Example:

Somewhat improve fitness: Climb ten mountains over 2000 feet.

Drastically improve fitness: Run a half marathon.

b. With the above information, now come up with ways you will improve these areas.

Example:

Climb 10 mountains:

Walk to work with weighted pack, climb

up and down the stairs in my house for ten minutes each day, go on a hike with some elevations once a week...

Run a marathon:

Start running two times per week and work up to more, get a static exercise bike to build up endurance, lose ten pounds...

# EFFORT AND CONFIDENCE.

*Is it a dream or a goal?*

You don't have to give a huge amount of effort to whatever adventures you decide to undertake. The amount of time and energy you will be required to donate will be up to you and be part of the holistic outlook of what your Adventure Audit uncovers.

For example, let's say you like the thought of climbing mountains and have the time, budget, fitness and locality to do so, but lack the desire to go to the efforts involved in making it happen. This would mean you should modify your goals to meet your desired effort output. Rather than climbing mountains, you deconstruct *why* you wanted to do it *(see chapter: Why do you want it?)* and figure a way to get close to meeting your requirements (scenery at height, great photos, challenging, etc) which involves a level of effort you are willing to put in, such as; easier hills and high points, driving to high areas for hikes, visiting mountains with trail cars to the top or even climbing just a portion of a hill (it's perfectly acceptable to not get to the top!)

*Sometimes the thought or idea of doing something is stronger than the desire to actually do it.*
*In this case, it's a dream, not a goal.*

If you think you really want to do something but would struggle to give the effort or you severely lack the confidence, you will only be setting yourself up to fail. Be honest with the effort you are currently willing to give to get a better Adventure Audit result. As you continue on your journey and become more experienced and confident, you may be happy to increase your effort levels, but for now be sure you're writing an effort check you're confident your circumstances will allow you can cash in.

From my experience as an adventure coach, one the

most common roadblocks to folk getting outdoors is a lack of confidence, but perhaps not the confidence to do the things you may expect. Most don't struggle with the confidence to do the outdoors adventures you may first imagine, such climb a mountain, go for their first camping trip or sign up to an indoor bouldering class – the biggest problem for most is simply *getting out the door.* There's a lot of fear to overcome to take the leap, to have/get the right gear, be sure your plans are correct, make the journey, find parking and simply dealing with your fear of possible danger. Oftentimes, the hike or activity is the easiest part!

If you lack confidence for certain things and right now do not want to push yourself, that's absolutely fine and perfectly acceptable. You will gain more confidence as you go, but just know you never have to push yourself outside of your comfort zone if you don't want to. One thing to note is that it is completely normal to be nervous beforehand.

I personally get nervous before every hike and outdoor activity – it's normal, so don't think you're alone. I once received a great piece of advice from someone who said, 'the feeling you get from being nervous is the same feeling you get from being excited', which is surprisingly true!

Some of the most toxic types of content which infect social media are those which encourage folk who are struggling to push themselves to reach far beyond what they are capable of in a tough love, no excuses way. It's usually the clichéd alpha male type asking, 'what's your excuse' as they shout about how they push themselves to the extreme everyday by getting up at 4:30 am, doing unnecessary amounts of exercise, working every waking minute and having no social life. Folk who live like this are usually masking some sort of pain, similar to how I was. They create pain to escape pain and struggle to understand why others can't just do as they do.

Here's what confidence in adventure really is –

*Having control over your ego to the extent you're happy to participate in your own journey and not comparing yourself what other people are doing in theirs.*

# EXERCISE 8.

## How Much Effort You Want To And Can Give.

Based on the answers you give, decide if you should cut, keep or change any goals.

a. Review your goals list and consider or take notes on just how much effort each goal will require you to give in the areas of time, physical, mental and financial. This will guide you to learn if you are truly willing and more importantly, able to make them happen.

Example:

Go on a 100-mile cycle:

Large effort on all fronts. I'll have to get a bike, plan the route, commit to multiple training cycles per week, deal with hostile drivers, will have to take time away from family.

Result: (Change) I don't think I actually want to give that amount of effort. I should plan a 50-mile cycle instead.

b.  From your goals list, note the areas related to your goals you feel confident in undertaking or learning.

Example:

Hiking, visiting new places.

c.  Now do the same with areas related to your goals you **don't** feel confident in undertaking or learning (yet)

Example:

Climb a mountain ridge, wildcamping.

d.  From the list you don't feel comfortable with, decide if you genuinely **want** to get to a place in which you feel confident to do them.

Example:

(Climb a mountain ridge)

Although I want to do this, I am actually terrified of the risk and the thought of leaving behind my loved ones. I realise now I am fine with not being confident in that area. I do not want to overcome my fears. Therefore, I have to modify my goals to accept this fact.

(Wildcamping)
This does scare me, and I have very low confidence, but I do want to pursue it and attempt to gain the knowledge and confidence required.

*It's okay to not want to or have to overcome a fear!*

# BUDGET.

*Nothing is free.*

A common misconception about hiking and the outdoors is that it is free.

There are ways it can absolutely be done for a low cost or with what you already have, but it will never be free. You will find it is mostly the elements, location and grander goals which force you into spending money, despite how hard you try not to.

Good hiking boots don't come cheap, waterproof gear is needed if you hike in anything but dry weather, (you should really still have waterproofs regardless, just in case), travel to locations costs money, extra food, portable phone chargers for emergencies, emergency accessories and more.

*For gear recommendations and a full list of what you may need for your adventures, see the chapter, 'Gear' and check out https://TartanHiker.com/gear .*

If you're on a tight budget or even have zero money to spend at the beginning or as you progress, don't worry - we will simply design a plan which requires less/no financial investment – but it will be a further factor in filtering down your adventures to fit the realities and preferences of your lifestyle. If you have dreams of winter mountaineering, but don't have the budget for gear, travel and such, you will have to let go of that dream and pivot to another. We are looking to design a completely attainable and realistic adventure life, so if you don't have the money, you'll have to modify your plans accordingly.

Note: dreams you have to let go of due to your Adventure Audit are not gone forever, just for now. You can audit yourself again if things change in the near or distant future.

# EXERCISE 9.

## How Much Money Can You Afford To Or Want To Spend On Your Adventure Plans.

Based on the answers you give, decide if you should cut, keep or change any goals.

a. Create a 'buy, borrow, have' list to help keep track of the following:
b. Do some research to find out what costs you may incur for the adventure goals you have planned and do a rough costing for each. Also note what you think you may be able to borrow and also what you already have (For help on gear costings and examples, check out https://TartanHiker.com/gear)
c. Now you have a rough idea of costings, consider and calculate if you can afford these pursuits or if you are willing to spend the funds required. Note that your budget can change as you progress, and some things may have a high 'get into' cost (such as camping), but once the gear is acquired, costs lower dramatically.

Example:

Go on an overnight camp in the wild:

Buy: Tent £129, Sleeping mat £99, Sleeping bag £80

Borrow: Stove, Headlamp

Have: Camping chair, old sleeping bag, backpack

# TIME AVAILABILITY.

*There's no point setting goals you won't have time to pursue.*

Perhaps the most important pillar to determine is how much time you can give to adventure. Knowing how much time you can give will help home in on your adventure plans and be the great eliminator!

You can properly plan and reveal what's available to you when you know how much time you can give. If you can give 30 minutes per day during the week, one hour on Saturday and three hours on Sunday, you will then have a blank space with adventure time 'buckets' to fill. For example, if you want to go on a hike you saw online which takes four hours - you won't be able to as you don't have the time allowance, which may seem obvious, but becomes clear upfront with set time allocations. Perhaps you see one which is two hours long, but a one hour drive each way – can't do it! You'll then start to filter down to what you *can* do regularly instead and fit in any longer efforts in when you have more time available, such as a once-a-month bigger hike.

If you have more time to spare, it doesn't mean you have to give it to adventure. You must simply decide how much you *want* to give.

Being pressed for and/or protective of your time means being realistic and putting down in writing what you're able to commit in order to make your adventure plans outlook clearer and achievable.

You must also be aware that you don't just give time to the execution of the adventure, you also have to give time to the planning, preparing, research, driving, parking, getting dressed, margin for error, fitness levels and more. Always be cautiously conservative about how long an adventure will take. If you get your times wrong, it will only lend to adding stress and could put you off future endeavours.

# EXERCISE 10.

## How Much Time You Can Or Will Realistically Commit.

Based on the answers you give, decide if you should cut, keep or change any goals.

a. Figure how much time you could allocate to adventuring and the 'behind the scenes' planning that it involves. What are your time buckets for your average week and can you give more time at various points in the month?

Example:

Two hours per day Mon-Fri.

Three hours Saturday.

Two hours Sunday.

Eight hour adventure once every two weeks.

Overnight adventure two days per month.

One week-long adventure once per year.

b. Now compare your time buckets with your goals and determine if you realistically have the time available to pursue your planned goals or if you have to cut, keep or change them. Remember to include not just the activity, but also the planning and research involved to make it happen.

Example:

Join an indoor bouldering club.

Realistic time required: 20 mins driving each way (40 mins), 20 mins getting ready (60 mins), 60 mins practise (2 hours)

Result: KEEP.

# LOCATION.

*Adventure is close, no-matter where you are.*

In my many years as a hiker and adventure coach, I've yet to meet a single person who dreams of epic adventures in the place they live. The adventure fantasies usually involve travel to a wild, unfamiliar land. It is understandable, but it should not be your first thought when dreaming of outdoor adventures. The key to an adventurous life is removing the obstacles and barriers in your way to make it as regularly accessible and as seamless as possible. A major time drain for adventures is getting to the start point then getting home, something which will shape your adventure future as we progress. Regardless of where you live, you must first seek out local adventure within as short a radius as possible, with further excursions being a factored-in treat and way to expand your skills on occasion.

If you wanted to drive to a mountain range, hiking area or to an outdoor adventure that is fifty miles away – you are therefore saying there are no-other adventures to be had within that 50-mile radius. You will then spend fifty miles driving by endless adventures, adding time, money and effort to the cost of your adventure which could be had locally.

A major example of this for visitors to Scotland is the Isle of Skye, a large island on the west-coast with incredible areas of beauty. Folk come to Scotland and spend hours and hundreds of miles driving by and ignoring some of the most beautiful areas on earth and mainland Scotland just to get to this one place which is crammed with tourists it doesn't have the ability or infrastructure to deal with, is almost always dealing with awful weather, is plagued by insects, involves driving everywhere and has become very expensive.

The areas local to you change year-round and are a place where you can make lasting and revisit-able memories, know where you are and have the chance to really get to know somewhere very well, even grow old with - rather than constantly drip-feeding yourself single-serve dips into areas you will never return to.

I'm not saying for a second you shouldn't plan to explore the length and breadth of the country, of course you can – just consider them a part of your plan and not *the* plan. Think of going further afield as being like a big purchase you make now and then, and your regular adventure areas like regular, affordable buys. Spend your location budget wisely to get a balanced, realistic, fulfilling adventure life.

When deciding how location will shape your adventure plans, you must determine if the areas you want to enjoy are actually necessary and/or possible given your budget, time and transport options. You may dream of climbing Ben Hope (the furthest north 3000 feet+ mountain in Scotland), but does your current circumstances lend to that being a possibility or is time to re-evaluate and find something closer?

# EXERCISE 11.

## Define Where You Can Adventure Regularly That Suits Your Circumstances.

Based on the answers you give, decide if you should cut, keep or change any goals.

    *a.*    *What distance/radius can you reasonably and regularly travel to when taking into account your transport options, desires, time and budget?*

Example:

One hour drive in any direction from Glasgow

    *b.*    *What areas are available within this travel zone?*

Example:

Loch Lomond, Stirling, Kilpatrick Hills, Clyde Muirshel National Park…

    *c.*    *Where do you want to visit that is outside this radius?*

Example:

Glencoe.

d. *How often could you visit the areas you desire that are outside of your regular radius?*

Example:

Once per month.

# SOCIAL DESIRES.

*Go it alone or nah?*

It's time to talk pals. Most hikers and adventure seekers tend to go with someone when heading to the outdoors, which is great, but you will have to accept compromise on what you want to achieve if you are going to rely on others joining your journey. You will have to align schedules, desires, risk levels, budgets, travel and a whole host of other factors. Be aware that when you are setting goals which involve other people, the achievement of those goals is reliant on a third party, and you will need to hope they want the same things as you. If you're fine with this and it still allows your goals to be planned and executed accordingly, that's perfect, work it into your plans. If it will make your adventure plans too difficult for your liking or impossible, it may be time to plan more solo endeavours into your new adventure life.

Going alone poses its own problems, such as safety issues when in isolated areas, a lack of motivation to get started or keep to plans, having no-one to push you on through difficult physical pursuits, loneliness and more. For these reasons it may very well be worth sacrificing certain goals and desires that you cannot get anyone to join you on.

If you want some company but don't have that special 'hiking buddy' to join you or if you don't have much of a friend group (or any friends), try searching Facebook and Meetup.com groups.

Or even better, bring your dog! (Or get one).

# EXERCISE 12.

## Decide How Much And If You Want To Involve Other People In Your Adventures.

Based on the answers you give, decide if you should cut, keep or change any goals.

If you don't want your adventure plans to involve a social aspect, skip this exercise.

a. From your goals list, decide which activities, if any you would like to involve other people in.

b. (If you have friends you think or know would be interested)

Make a list of those friends and pitch them your idea(s) when you complete your Adventure Audit.

c. (If you don't have friends, or friends who may be interested)

Research and arrange to join or get involved with groups to make connections or invite along.

# REVIEW.

*Let's make sure.*

You should now have a comprehensive list of all the goals you believe you can realistically achieve, having been through the Adventure Audit process. It is important that you do not progress to the next section until you are absolutely certain you are happy with the goals you have set, and you have run them all thoroughly through all audit questions. Ask again if you need to cut, keep or change any goals.

# EXERCISE 13.

1. Review your answers one last time before proceeding to the next step.

# IT'S TIME FOR ACTION.

*Goals without actions are dreams.*

You will now break down your goals into actionable steps which fit into your daily life. Even though you now have a clear vision of what you want and your goals are written down, they are of no use unless you take action! You will create clear steps to fit your goals into your schedule, injecting daily adventure into your life with constant small wins which serve your near and long-term goals.

## *Action steps for your goals list.*

Each goal you have set will now be given **five actionable steps** which will help in making it a reality. Set a mixture of bigger steps that will take time, and small steps you can tick off without great effort. There may/will be more than five steps required, but setting too many actions can easily intimidate and confuse you, while making your goal seem further away than it really is. Importantly, set a 'ball rolling' step which will get you started. Regardless of how small you may think it is, if you at least do *something* to take you closer to your goal, you will now have some momentum and will be on your way. It matters not how ridiculously small it is, it's about getting started!

Example goal: Go on a three-night, long-distance camping hike.

Actionable steps:

**Ball-rolling step**

1. Buy a set of tent pegs.
2. Make a complete gear list with costings that fit my budget.
3. Decide where I want to go and plan the route.
4. Ask friends and family if I can borrow any of the required gear.
5. Go on an easy overnight camp at a campsite for practice.

Once you do this, your goals will now be brought to life and serve as a navigational aid toward finally achieving your dream adventures. No stone is left unturned, and no unreasonable goals will remain to potentially block your path.

Note: Once you complete and tick-off an action step, add a new one in its place until eventually there's no more steps to add and your goal is achieved.

# EXERCISE 14.

## Bring Your Goals To Life With Steps.

1. To each goal, add five or more actionable steps toward achieving your goal, including a small, super-easy step to get the ball rolling.

Note: You may want to write each goal and action steps on a single page of your notebook each, so when you tick off an action step you have plenty of space to add more!

# GEAR.

---

*All the gear...*

---

Gear will depend on your choice of adventure and your budget. The following is a list of the most common items pretty much everyone would benefit from having for outdoor pursuits. This is the gear you will most likely need in an ideal world for most outdoor adventure journeys at a basic level for comfort and improved safety. The gear you choose will depend on the type of adventure you are going to undertake according to your plan and budget.

You do not NEED specialist gear for a lot of adventure pursuits, but it helps. Don't worry if you can't afford them!

The page on my site linked below goes more in depth for additional gear for things such as bigger hikes, camping and more, plus of course my content has hundreds of videos offering my gear advice.

Common recommended gear for hiking:
- Hiking boots
- Base layer t-shirt
- Mid layer t-shirt
- Top layer fleece
- Waterproof jacket or poncho
- Waterproof trousers
- Merino wool (or blend) socks
- Charging bank for phone (ideally two)
- Backpack (at least 20 litres day pack to 45 litres, likely more if camping)
- First aid pack
- Water filter

Common recommended gear for camping:
- Tent
- Sleeping mat
- Sleeping bag (type varies by season)
- Stove and gas
- Headlight
- Water filter

I will include a link to my beginner adventurer gear

recommendation page below and will stick mostly to Amazon for ease of purchasing. There are many other places you can source gear, but as everyone has ease of access to Amazon, it is a great place to start, and beginner gear purchased from there is of great quality with the returns being super easy.

There are also several codes for money off which I have arranged or found online which work at the time of writing. They are not listed here as products change, become discontinued or have quality lessened over time. Discount codes also run out, therefore with an external page on my website, I can keep it up to date for you.
https://tartanhiker.com/gear/

Another wonderful source of outdoors gear are charity/thrift shops and sites such as DePop, Vinted and eBay.

# WORK WITH ME.

*You + me = good times!*

If you'd like to go deeper or work with me directly, here's a brief overview of the services I currently offer:

- **Found Outside Adventure Audit Video Course.** The core content of this book is also available as a video course, presented by me. Ideal if you prefer visual or guided learning.

- **Adventure Coaching (Monthly. Online).** I am your adventure coach. Together we will plan adventure into your schedule, and I will be available to answer your questions. I'll guide you on what to do, when and how, keep you motivated and on track in your new adventure life. We will work together closely to achieve and maintain a wonderful life of adventure and on-occasion (for an additional fee), go on adventures together in the highlands of Scotland.

- **Adventure Coaching (One-Off Sessions).**
Due to a consistently full schedule and waiting list, recurring monthly coaching is rarely available—so these sessions are designed to deliver maximum clarity and value in one go, in which I help you build the perfect adventure, plan your trip to Scotland, or dive into any topic you need guidance on.

- **Adventure Planning & 'Get Into' Sessions.**
These are tailored one-off sessions where I help you build the perfect adventure, plan your trip to Scotland, or dive into any topic you need guidance on.

- **'Get Into' Starter Sessions.**
One of the most popular offerings—these sessions are designed to help you get started with a new kind of adventure. I walk you through gear, logistics, mindset, and what to expect—eliminating all guesswork and overwhelm.

- **Adventure Audit Reviews.**
If you'd like expert feedback on your completed Adventure Audit, or want help working through

the process, I offer guided review sessions.

- **Guided adventure.**
A premium service, I will plan and guide you on an unforgettable adventure in the Highlands of Scotland, designed to your requirements.

- **Social Media Coaching for Outdoor Creators.**
I provide tailored advice for aspiring outdoor influencers—helping you refine your content strategy, improve your channel and content, and build a sustainable career around the outdoors.

For more on all of these, visit: https://tartanhiker.com

# A FINAL WORD.

---

Get found outside*!*

---

Never be held hostage to your goals. If you are working hard toward an outcome, but on the journey you realise 'actually, this isn't want I want anymore', then quit. Walk away. I can tell you from experience that I have made the mistake of following the 'never quit no matter what' attitude far too many times in my life which led me way down the wrong path. Perhaps the best piece of advice I could offer anyone not just in their pursuit of adventure, but in life, is that it's okay to change your mind - it's okay to quit.

If something is just too hard and is stressing you out, be sure to ask yourself what hurts most – the stress of continuing, or the disappointment of not achieving the goal. Some great things are just not worth the payoff. You can retake the Adventure

Audit at any point if you feel you're not quite on the right path.

The most important takeaway of this book though, is that this journey is your own. Do not compare or create yours based on those you look up to.

The pursuit of outdoor happiness is a lifelong adventure that will never be completed.

You outdoors journey starts from the wild within.

I'll see you out there.

Paul.